LAMPLIGHTER

LAMPLIGHTER

POEMS

S. A. MCNUTT

Copyright © 2024 by Stephanie A. McNutt

All rights reserved.

No part of this book may be reproduced in any form or by any electronic or mechanical means, including information storage and retrieval systems, without written permission from the author, except for the use of brief quotations in a book review.

❦ Created with Vellum

For my Husband,
For my Mom, and Dad

CONTENTS

Introduction   ix

PART ONE
Nature Poems

Lamplighter	3
Childhood	5
Little Waters	7
10,000	11
Summer Meets Fall	13
Yellow, the Color of Happiness	15
Breeding Ground	17
Sunday Afternoon	19
Attention!	21
The Unofficial Poetry Community, #519	23
Disquiet	25
Skinny in the Moonlight	27
Lightening, River, Path	29
Wormhole	31
Silence in the Desert	33
Matchbox	35
Shine Like Stars	37
Path Through Darkness	39
Author Notes	41

PART TWO
Sound Poems

Oneliner	51
House of Mirth	53
Raven Haired	55
Glorious Refrain	57
Covenant of Peace	59
A Poet's Right	61
Lately	63
Umbrella Man	65

May 3rd	67
Half the Man	69
The Professor	71
We Are Tired	73
Arlington	75
Heart Tax	77
A Moment is Centuries	79
Sunshine and Moon	81
Author Notes	83

PART THREE
On Writing

Papaya	93
Diligence	95
Stories	97
Meal for Baby	99
Love	101
We Doubt	103
Mouthpiece	105
Levez-vous	107
Ink	109
Not Goodbye	111
Hammer and Nail	113
Author Notes	115
Acknowledgments	121
About the Author	123

INTRODUCTION

Welcome to Lamplighter.

Lamplighter is named after the first poem in the book, inspired by my life growing up on a small Minnesotan lake. These poems reflect the journey I've been on these past 20-plus years.

In 20 years, I've grown as a writer and poet. I want to say I've arrived with some clarity, but I haven't. Sure, some things are clear. The important things are clear. Yet, as the years go by, I have more experiences and questions to sift through.

The curious nature is unsatisfied. I remain curious and open to every new adventure. This is my beginning.

I am honored to share my poetry with you.

Blessings,
    S. A. McNutt

PART ONE

NATURE POEMS

The following poems in this section directly or indirectly reflect the natural world. Many are childhood reflections and memories of living on a lake. Some memories are like gossamer strands captured from retellings of stories I've heard.

As a country girl, I had a country girl's life. I climbed trees and watched sunsets from the boughs of an old Oak. In one way or another, I am returning to that shore, that tree, hoping to have another glimpse at the past.

The themes in these poems are like luminaries, like a mirror to look through. Poetry is the lens that helps me focus and refine things I've believed about myself. Through them, I hope to see more clearly.

LAMPLIGHTER

Lamplighter lights the sphere
well before the night is here,
through which I see the sky
swallowing up my eye.

A great womb is holding me,
part of the cosmic heredity.
The lake fish and I
are born again a second time.

Right where the water breaks,
what the fish can't, I forsake-
The green mossy afterbirth
on the shores of this earth.

(April 18, 2008)

CHILDHOOD

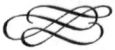

The lexical entry of me:
A lake where I lived
swimming with fish
under rippling glass.

A career of collecting bullfrogs
for bait
at a nickel apiece,
thrown into an empty
mint chocolate chip
gallon ice cream pail.

Bridge Troll was played
with cousins on lazy Sundays
between the weekend neighbors
and Grandma's.

We took turns being
the villainous troll.

S. A. MCNUTT

* * *

Grandmother liked me
well, enough for a stranger,
but thought me odd when
my fashion sensibility
refused a washcloth bathing suit.

I had a sense of pride
at four, practically an adult.

My own was
in my dresser drawer
across the lake.

Organ playing was a particular
talent of Grandma's,
played once at
the Frog Bar in Arizona.

She had a specialty of Fox Trots and dancing on
bar tops in high heels.

She married a hard life of farming,
a Depression life
set to the sound of war.

My Grandfather celebrated the
end while leaving her to milk
the cows by candlelight,
and no radio to herald
a celebration of 1945.

LITTLE WATERS

I.
10,000 deposits of liquid sky
from where the land rises up.

The loon mellows
its sorrow in the morning.

I am a stranger here--
in the land that breastfed me
on honeysuckles
under front porch steps.

II.
The cold steel sky
glints -- scrapes and
pillages the gray dome,
holding it in,
a rain-globe shaken
as the city greets me back.

And rising before me,
drained of color,
hills and skeleton houses
of bleached doors,
eternal beds.

The flag billows
with a night full of stars
to hide the deeds of war.

The flag shivers
and blood runs
like stripes over--
courage of pure white.

The stones skipped
on waves of grass.
They build up forts
to play in,
for boys in feathered caps.

III.
Barbie dolls domesticate
the girl inside.
She climbs the oak tree,
waiting to be rescued
under sherbet orange,
prairie pink,
skinned-my-knee
sunsets.

IV.
I am dry.

I am brittle.
I am parched of these waters
my veins, long rooted, fed.

The pools, the puddles--
my mirrors.
To see my aging face,
and see the eternal,
to hear eternal echoes
of the whole world
ripple out from
a single drop of time.

The whole of everything
shared in my reflection.
We are caught between
water and sky.

10,000

Ten thousand bricks
and every reason why
to shatter the illusion,
glass rippling against the sky.

We had our reasons—
Someone came for a visit,
gave us tools for supplies.

Ten thousand hands
clasped together against
towers, and powers,
and promises of entreaty.

We had our moment—
Our platform to rally
of wailing and weeping.

Ten thousand faces
walking alone as one

on Lake Street in the city,
home for the motherless.

We had our comforts
burn up in a night,
illusion of safety gone.

Ten thousand ripples
in ten thousand lakes,
and ten thousand places,
where my heart aches.

SUMMER MEETS FALL

Fall blows on me
from the West.
Summer flirts with me
from the East.

I am between past and future
with warm kisses sweet—
a jealous and experienced lover
-- my parvenu
forces its warmth away,
eclipses the passion,
   blows back its passionate verse
   on a freshly laid page.

Leaves fall
and talk to me
of this changing course and tide.
The chill embraces me
and holds me with amber arms,

> waiting for the green man to come
> many months from now.

YELLOW, THE COLOR OF HAPPINESS

Sometimes as obvious as bright flowers peaking in green fields,
dispersed little faces among the many shafts of grass.

Sometimes diffused, rays of sunlight, sparkling and bright, on everything it touches.

You are all those happinesses to me while dancing.

BREEDING GROUND

Love is a desperate, tender thing
that breaks forth towards the sun,
a shoot out of dry ground.

It is a miracle of forgiving
pliable earth, and tender rain,
and of nitrogen and phosphates.

Love gains the tender soil,
spreading a veil of leaves
to dapple the land
in a mosaic of light.

It does groan with blooming reds,
all colors like fireworks shouting,
tickling the air
with joy
and tenderness.

(June 1, 2022)

SUNDAY AFTERNOON

2 cups of white porcelain.
Big band strikes up for practice
at the Colorado
School for the Blind.
A crooner carries distant memories
from times of war.
Sun is blushing behind
Mount Evans,
deepening the blue of leaves.
The edge of the mountains
is fire-tipped with orange.
French pressed twice over.
Cream and sugar in the cup.
Singers' voices intertwine.
Moon River breaks our hearts.
It rises up, then cup to lips rise too
with our coffee at sunset.

(April 13, 2008)

ATTENTION!

Attention! Attention! An Emergency has been
   detected in the building!

Darkness, not silently tonight
   but fiercely with a giant tug,
   covers like heavy wool
   blanketing us in.

Sun comes with a crackle,
   burns its edges.

The night, the night
is for the artist.
Fierce are the strokes
of her brush
across the canvas.

Night is quick
and deepens before the light.

S. A. MCNUTT

> The song of the light is greater
> -- it shines,
> and the darkness fails
> to understand it.
>
> (October 19, 2000)

THE UNOFFICIAL POETRY COMMUNITY, #519

Rage on
flaring embers
of burning night,
your right to pain
is to fight.

DISQUIET

Mine is the disquiet
that bankrupts peace
And steals
the furniture of comfort.
Hope and promise
speak in dulcet tones,
and in the wake of their silence
they are emptied of the future.

In dark corners, whispers
land like needles on the skin
threading these tiny hairs
like a net,
and I am caught up.

A guppy netted
and bowled for decoration.

Or is it a tapestry?
One that threads its way,

knitting me together again
like a highway of conversation
singing through every part of me.

I am a hum
and a buzz.

Nothing remains silent in me.

(Sept. 10, 2019)

SKINNY IN THE MOONLIGHT

We submerged –
Ripples and twilight sky,
    goose skin prickled,
    hands raised in the air

pulling at threads of moonlight
woven between fingers.
We played cat's cradle.

We dove down into the deep dark,
grasping at rocks
in spawning beds.

(May 25, 2022)

LIGHTENING, RIVER, PATH

Lightning hits the tree.
Rivers are changing their course,
the path I must follow.

WORMHOLE

Her voice flowed against
strands of chestnut brown hair
blowing in the wind–
my name across
our neighbor's yard.

For lunch.
For dinner.
For bed.

I went out as a child,
came in as an adult.

Light of a silver moon
met hands raised in prayer
diving into a surface
of rippling tides
tickling the water.

My past.

S. A. MCNUTT

    My present.
    My future.

    I dove in as a child,
    emerged as an adult.

    (May 22, 2022)

SILENCE IN THE DESERT

We fell into the silence of the desert,
landing on the red-hot sand.
It burned like coals on our back.

Hands entwined, pointing at Virgo, ruling queen
    of the onyx-colored night sky pricked with
    light.

How long did it take to poke holes in the veil?
    Light was behind the barrier sky.
Without it, we would be undone.

"Money grows in the desert." You whispered.
Behind a halo of neon signs pointed their arrows
    above us.

"We don't need money," I replied, trying to shut
    out the signs drawing us to their light.

You tugged my hand, leading me to where fire burns away the night in an artificial glow. The screams of despair and merriment blanket the coyote's howl.

MATCHBOX

She had a graveyard in her heart.
Graves the size of matchboxes.
Avoidance preserved
her peace for a time,
until the tears would
make their way.
They were the irrigation
of her garden,
but the bitterness was too acidic
for anything to grow,

and so, she reconciled
to tending the graves.

SHINE LIKE STARS

Not enough to disappear,
but dark enough.
Not enough to shine,
but buffed enough
and glowing.

Not enough to stand alone
on empty streets.
A threat to who?
Me or you?

I am not enough to disappear
into the night,
or shine like stars
of innumerable light.

PATH THROUGH DARKNESS

We left the darkness
in our rearview mirror.
Staying the course,
we took the northern route.
Everything at our backs,
we moved to a new horizon,
to that line above the ocean.
Highway of the sun,
and we were drawn forward.
Everything we knew, behind.

AUTHOR NOTES

PART ONE

NOTES ON LAMPLIGHTER

I grew up on a small lake in Minnesota. Lake imagery and water are infused in my writing. The first poem, Lamplighter, reflects the theme of what G.K. Chesterton meant when he said, "There are two ways of getting home, and one of them is to stay there. The other is to walk round the whole world till we come back to the same place …"

LAMPLIGHTER IS about two worlds contained in one sphere. One existed when I dove deep into the lake and visited the world of Sunfish. The other world existed above the surface when I broke free. I could exist again in my world, but the fish could not, and the sky's dome held us together.

S. A. MCNUTT

NOTES ON CHILDHOOD

Childhood is a poetic snapshot of days. The ones spent at my grandmother's house stood out. She lived across the lake from us. Sometimes, we drove there, and other times, we would take a pontoon boat. We were there for Friday night chicken dinner most weeks.

As the poem progresses, I recall my grandmother sitting at her organ, teaching me the foxtrot. There are parts within the poem that live between memory and imagination, bits collected from stories my father and grandmother shared. The last stanza is from one of his memories.

My father is a natural storyteller. His memory weaves into the poem right at the point when WWII ended. He was a little boy working in a field with his father and brother when a local police officer came and told them the war was over.

In *A Tale of Two Cities*, Charles Dickens writes, "A wonderful fact to reflect upon, that every human creature is constituted to be that profound secret and mystery to every other." Grandma, My Father, and I are still a mystery, and so are we all, revealed page by page.

NOTES ON LITTLE WATERS

As one might expect, *Little Waters* opens with the idea of water. The opening line references Minnesota, the land of 10,000 lakes. It is followed by the image of the solitary loon, Minnesota's state bird.

. . .

The stanzas progress as a reflection of a return visit to my "homeland." It carries the tension of memory and present reality, the idea that "You can't return home again."

The poem exists out of a longing to be a little girl again and stand on the shore of my childhood lake. This poem will never truly be finished as long as I can return.

NOTES ON 10,000

We return to Minnesota's motto, "The Land of 10,000 Lakes." *Ten thousand* acts like a banner that many Minnesotans can understand. The poem is a lament from my heartbreak for my home state during the 2020 riots.

I prefer to focus on the reality of what's left. Heartache does not have an easy answer. It is repaired with immense cost.

NOTES ON SUMMER MEETS FALL

The expression best fitting this poem is "winds of change." It is the warmth on one side of your face and cool air on the other. It is like sitting between two seasons: Summer to Fall and Winter to Spring. It is a distinct moment where one season yields to the dominion of the other.

The mythology of the Green Man is layered within the context of this poem. The legend is surrounded by pagan and Christian traditions, like Sir Gawain and the Green Knight, which loosely influenced the idea behind this poem.

NOTES ON YELLOW, THE COLOR OF HAPPINESS

Is happiness a color? My friend once said that happiness is like the color yellow. It was a revelation. Yellow feels like the only happy color. I see it in the bright wildflowers bursting in fields. I see it in the sun, which faithfully shines, bringing warmth and new days. It is a golden hour of happiness.

NOTES ON BREEDING GROUND

Breeding Ground is an extended metaphor for growing love. It is the place where love grows in rich and fertile soil. Love needs nurturing, like plants needing sunlight.

As LOVE GROWS, it creates shelter for those it loves. Like a plant that produces flowers or changes leaves, love expresses its fullness in joy. It is a good fruit and a bounty for many.

NOTES ON SUNDAY AFTERNOON

*Sunday Afternoo*n is written from the memory of many Sundays spent like this one, listening to the Glen Miller Swing band practice at the School for the Blind. We would listen as the sun set behind the Rocky Mountains, drinking our French press coffee.

NOTES ON ATTENTION!

Nothing about this date is significant, nor about the poem or why I wrote it. It was Denver. The Millennium scare of January

1st was behind us.

Less than a year after I wrote this poem, the poem took on new significance. Now, a simple glowing sunset reflects a different fire burning and a new emergency like 9/11. I don't see the same poem or think of the memory in the same light. September 11th, 2001, changed how I will forever view this poem and memory.

NOTES ON THE UNOFFICIAL POETRY COMMUNITY, #519

This poem was inspired by an exercise in the forum called the Unofficial Poetry Community. "Rage on flaring embers of the burning night" talks about the tension between the warmth of a flame and light. The closer you get to the flame, the greater the risk of being burned.

NOTES ON DISQUIET

Anxiety often robs us of the comfort we would otherwise have in our environments. We are unable to rest. We are alert to potential dangers surrounding us. Our insecurities rob us of our real value and worth.

Whether real or not, we may think others are talking behind our backs. It feeds our insecurities as we imagine others have discovered our weakest selves. The prickling of goosebumps on the skin reveals the danger of having the worst parts of ourselves revealed.

. . .

S. A. MCNUTT

By the end of the poem, there is a reclamation of control. We take control of our thoughts and our beliefs about ourselves. Maybe those whispers weren't someone talking behind your back, but they were the hum of activity within yourself. Every sound within you breaking that silence is also keeping you alive.

NOTES ON SKINNY IN THE MOONLIGHT

When you grow up on a lake, skinny dipping feels like a rite of passage – and not as scandalous as it may seem. This poem uses contrasting images related to childhood and growing up. I used the game "Cat's Cradle," juxtaposed next to fish spawning beds.

As a rite of passage from youth to adulthood, it touches on the age of the Garden of Eden before Adam and Eve were clothed. It pays homage to childhood. It reflects on our innocence, but it's removed from the image of shame.

NOTES ON LIGHTENING, RIVER, PATH

This poem is a Haiku that ties the natural elements to the idea of change. Lightning strikes in an instant. Follow a river long enough, and inevitably, it will change course. An instantaneous moment can lead to a life-altering change that redirects everything moving forward. Change is our one constant.

NOTES ON WORMHOLE

Imagine a wormhole bending time in strange ways. It's like wind moving over the earth, shaping hard-fixed things by etching the surface of time. This wormhole compresses certain moments and continues to repeat them through the years.

LAMPLIGHTER

. . .

Whenever my mother called my name for lunch as a kid, it now seems like her voice will forever carry on the wind and echo through time. Memories play on repeat from childhood to adulthood; some memories will skip like a scratched record that I can no longer repair. This is my wormhole.

NOTES ON SILENCE IN THE DESERT

The trap is set in the heat of the desert, and the false oasis awaits. A trip through Las Vegas one night is part of the inspiration for this poem—a juxtaposition between the darkness of the desert and the glow of false light from the city.

The other influence is Vanity Fair, as seen in John Bunyan's *Pilgrim's Progress*. "Moreover, at this fair, there is at all times to be seen jugglings, cheats, games, plays, fools, apes, knaves, rogues, and that of every kind."

NOTES ON MATCHBOX

It is an honest poem that deals with my struggle with infertility while imagining the shared struggle of many women through time. It is for the person with a private graveyard in their heart where they are the only visitor.

I offer this hope, "Sing, barren one, who has not given birth, burst into singing and shout, you who have not travailed. For more are the children of the desolate than the children of the married one," says *Adonai*." Isaiah 54:1

NOTES ON SHINE LIKE STARS

Have you struggled with the feeling of being overlooked? Shining like a star, a light in the darkness, it's that thing we desire when we seek to make a difference in the lives around us and be recognized for what we offer. Together, we become a city on the hill.

I HAVE no desire to burn brighter than others. I desire to be counted among the many, valued for the light I bring. This poem focuses on the worth and value we all offer.

NOTES ON PATH THROUGH DARKNESS

My husband and I moved during the Lockdowns of 2020. On our journey westward, I remember looking in the rearview mirror only to see a tornado forming in the background. The sky was dark, sickly green, and storming. There was a distinct line between the storm behind and the blue skies ahead. The sky in front of us was bathed in light, and it just happened to be the direction of our future.

"THE LIGHT SHINES in the darkness, but the darkness doesn't understand it." – John 1:5

PART TWO

SOUND POEMS

Poems and sounds go together like an ocean and a wave, intrinsic. Regarding sound techniques, I am a fan of alliteration, puns, and mellifluous words, which essentially means to flow with honey. I imagine these words dripping like honey over the tongue.

One of the best techniques for authentic sound in poetry is onomatopoeia, words that will pop and crunch their way into our ears. You will want to sound those out.

The poems selected for this section use this concept in various ways. Some may appear obvious and clear, while others land like a whisper in the ear. Every poem, on some level, relies on the nature of sound to relay its intent.

ONELINER

I use puns like I punch,
with intention!

HOUSE OF MIRTH

1ST VERSION

What is it worth,
this house of mirth
when at the door
life comes no more
and silence rings
and ears do sting,
the bell, they do abhor?

What is the sound
that goes around,
that rings the bell
throughout the town,
like a treasonous thing?

Is it a flaring timorous ring
that drowns the songs
the choirs sing,
like a murderous rogue?

Whose is the hand

that carries the force
to make the sound
of a mourners remorse,
like a bearded thug?

What is the beast
who adorns the feast
where meters meet
and greeters greet
like an infested rat?

This is the thing.
There is the rogue.
Here is the thug,
and see the rat that
pierced the sound
and stopped the ring
with the force of a feastly beast.

RAVEN HAIRED

Purloined kiss
on peach soft cheeks.
Crescent moon eyes
waxed in disbelief.

Raven black hair
Zephyrs take in flight.
Dancing led the marauder here--
both perplexed, stare.

Morse code-d words click,
utterance in fox trot,
out from under the left two
she in tango withdrew.

He, cricket legs hop
down sidewalks out of view.
Night sounds drowned loneliness--
just one, not two.

GLORIOUS REFRAIN

I met you on the baseline.
We rise like falsetto.
You are the instrument in the aria.

Between the scale
we are half notes,
undiscovered chords.

Through the ballad,
the rising chorus
resounds, O' Victory.

Glorious refrain
encountering the treble,
but for me— a silent opus.

Now alone, I the choir,
solo voce, sottovoce.
Diminished upon the coda.

COVENANT OF PEACE

Peace I'll lay down for
on this, my dower bed.
A covenant of kisses
on my head.

Peace I will dress
my best for,
white gown
dyed in river's red,
streams joined from
its fountainhead.

Peace I will
silence my tongue for,
a cup to pass
between me and you.

Peace I will lay down for,
under grassy hills

of harvest crest
silently, in final rest.

A POET'S RIGHT

I can write meter.
I can write rhyme.
I can feed you words,
line by line.

I can sing a song
and carry a tune
 to faraway lands,
cut in rocks like runes.

I can measure beats,
make words retreat.
Speed things forward,
and signal defeat.

I can make you feel,
and make us weep.
Share in sorrows,
hearts cut so deep.

S. A. MCNUTT

> I can up the start,
> wind down the end,
> light up the middle,
> this poet's your friend.
>
> (May 3, 2020)

LATELY

Johnny came dressed and ready
to disappear into the night,
his identity is hard to distinguish.

Johnny came ready to protest.
Our cause, already on his tongue.
But good ol' Johnny
had other plans.

Johnny came with matches
and money,
cried out
"Let the city burn."

"Whoa, watch yourself Johnny."
We cried, beginning
to be concerned.

Johnny came a leapin' and leading
out the charge

with words we'd never heard,
until the police came calling.

Johnny left us hanging.
No one's seen from him or heard,
and now we're the ones
they're detaining
for crimes of the violent
and disturbed.

"Where's Johnny?" We say.

"No one here by that name."
They reply.

"Oh look" I point
to the man in the corner
dressed in blue
and wearing a badge.

"That's him there, officer.
That's Johnny."

But he insisted
that it was not Johnny,
"No, That's Officer
John B. Lately, to you."

UMBRELLA MAN

No showers in the forecast and the weather's
   looking fine.
Where you goin', Umbrella Man? Can you spare
   the time?

What a riot? All these fun and games.
Check your gear and try to look the same.

No showers in the forecast and the weather's
   looking fine.
Where you goin', Umbrella Man? Can you spare
   the time?

Is that Billy's club? The one in your hand?
Power equals force times velocity in the land of
   Uncle Sam.

No showers in the forecast and the weather's
   looking fine.

S. A. MCNUTT

>Where you goin', Umbrella Man? Can you spare the time?

MAY 3RD

We build our world in silence.
A skeleton filled mirror,
Gasp,
"Should they escape
and divulge my fear?"
but remains
the noiseless vanity
in my ear
collapsing inside
the well-oiled drum
that beats in the chest
thumping, thumping, thumping
It thrills me and keeps me
within each breath
tapping, tapping, tapping
where hand holds wrist
to keep me here,
to greet me
with the absence of lips.

HALF THE MAN

I am half the man
with half the suit.
My grays don't match.
I am the middle road,
creeping towards the black.
The twill of my coat pills,
my pants are snagged,
my shoes wear me --
with a fancy braided edge.
I am care-worn,
travel-worn,
alone!
A meeting on Monday.
I fly in on Saturday
and make a vacation of it.
I carry my daughter in my pocket
from 4 years ago,
with braces.
I paid half
of her pretty smile.

S. A. MCNUTT

    I follow the line of un-preferred
    to lines of Dodge Stratus'--
    I prefer my room at the Holiday Inn.
    Then the key.
    Then the car.
    Something borrowed.
    Something blue.

THE PROFESSOR

He reads poetry like he smokes--
Deep inhaling breaths
with a whistling nose
filling up the holes in his chest.
Out with the sssssssss's
like a smokey strand,
wafting up, out, and in-
go the meter,
swallow the swelling rhyme
of menthol.
And buzz
of words upon the ears.
Rattling breath of
a man worth his weight in words.
And so, the traveling sentence
transfixes his mind with pleasure,
like the pleasure of a full cigarette
--only blunted
with the force of a word edit,

S. A. MCNUTT

        snuffed with the rejection of a line,
        put out is the meaning
        that lacks understanding
        of the words behind the rhyme.

WE ARE TIRED

My body lies me down
nightly, dirt over
my eyes -- tired,
and bright mornings
blind me. Heaviness
lifted for awhile
'till those water
deep puddles I tread
deepen. Ground sifting
and water's overhead.
I look for the baby blue
eyes in the sky kind of
freedom, my head above the
waters for a second. Clasp
a bit of air between my teeth
whose job it is to filter the
water some -- the air is not enough
before I am under again.
These are my days
of struggling.

ARLINGTON

Through Peter's gate we
just visiting say all,
young, old, Dead alike --
look on hills
crested like waves
with fields full of
tombstones, white.
Some chipped out
of existence by
wind with secrets
to which the Orioles
reply -- whip-poor-wills,
not their own will
but prompted from
the shadowed valley
saying,
"See here my deeds.
Look -- chirp, chirp, chirp.
I have taken them
down with me--

twee tut tut twee,
and paid my debt
over my eyes -- chirrup."
And we pass by --
Odes from Homeric birds
and take our pictures
by blank white teeth,
capturing war and peace,
that lies twain 'neath my feet.

(May 25, 2008)

HEART TAX

Dil Lagaan (Heart tax).
　　　Payment is due.

A MOMENT IS CENTURIES

(Hindi)
Ek pal sadiyaan hai
Hum pyaar nah mile

Yeh dard kaafi hai
Zindagi hum phir mile

(English)
A moment is centuries
We do not meet love

This pain is enough
Life we meet again

SUNSHINE AND MOON

(Hindi)
Dhoop se chaand mile
Iss khushi hum safar
Iss dil par
hum phir mile

(English)
Sunshine and moon meet,
　We travel this happiness.
On this heart
　we again meet.

AUTHOR NOTES

PART TWO

NOTES ON ONELINER

I love puns. Part of the clevernesses of puns is in the verbal gymnastics and mental twists used to intone the meaning. My use of sound and action conveys the image and idea in this single line. This single line creates a pugilistic punny poem without being a pun or punny. I intend to get every drop into a single image and line.

NOTES ON HOUSE OF MIRTH

I want to note that poems in this section are best read out loud, especially this one. This poem is my husband's favorite, and he has the first stanza memorized. It's strange to have someone quote your poetry to you. I am not sure I will get used to that idea. This is one of the earliest versions of *House of Mirth*, though there are many versions I've created. This was my first.

. . .

S. A. MCNUTT

SOME OF THE works that inspired this poem were John Donne's *For Whom the Bell Tolls*, the title of Earnest Hemingway's novel. More obviously, the title is directly inspired by Edith Wharton's *House of Mirth*. Thematically, however, the poem rests on Donne's influence, "And therefore never send to know for whom the bell tolls; It tolls for thee."

HOUSE OF MIRTH looks at our fear of death, its disruption to our lives, and the discomfort of it. The ending points to the Black Plague, representing that death is a common fear and that no one truly escapes. Though death may be an inescapable part of the human condition, it is unnatural and wrong. We were meant for something better, something permanent.

(ALSO NOTE, this was written years before Covid).

NOTES ON RAVEN HAIRED

I wrote this poem for my friend (you know who you are). She told me about a date that didn't go well. The way she described it to our group one coffee night out formed the poem above. It's an inside joke in some ways, but not just that; it is one story that represents the stories that filled our weekly coffee shop gatherings. We were four friends who consistently met each week for several years.

ON THE TECHNICAL SIDE, I played around with the sound by adding odd rhyming lines to aid in the meter of each stanza. The reader may have also noted my strong affinity for the use of "fox-trot" in other poems. This word connects to my Grandma (see *Childhood*) and her love of music and dancing. That musicality and playfulness in the poem hints at the location of the date, a Salsa Dancing Night. This aided in the dancing imagery I used throughout the stanzas.

NOTES ON GLORIOUS REFRAIN

What if we were a song— our lives were a song, a chorus, played by an orchestra? Would we be a masterpiece? *Glorious Refrain* picks up on the musical implications of a relationship. Each person in your life adds to the overall song. You remain the final refrain in the end. You are the final voice, a breath, and a whisper.

NOTES ON COVENANT OF PEACE

I want more poems about peace. It's what I desire for my life. The overarching idea of *Covenant of Peace* was inspired by Emily Dickinson's poem *I Died for Beauty* where she discusses beauty and truth being buried side by side. I considered the cost of peace and why it's so compelling that we would die for it. Ultimately, the idea of peace encompasses the image of the one who is called the Prince of Peace.

NOTES ON A POET'S RIGHT

Each poet has their own goal when writing a poem. They drive toward emotional content. Through technique, the poet moves towards emotional emphasis, both within and without.

WHAT IS the essence a poet tries to accomplish when writing a poem? Here, I mean it to be light and brief. The poem relies on shorter words to carry a quick pace throughout. It is for this reason that the sound, when read aloud, bounces playfully to the end.

NOTES ON LATELY

Johnny Come Lately, Provocateurs, and *Umbrella Men* (see the following poem) are used in the way the poem describes. The result of their actions should be well seen now. In the summer of 2020, we saw cities burning, people looting, and destruction all over the news. It is my belief that those mentioned in this poem were part of lighting the first match. They light the match and disappear. The city is in chaos. Those left behind are arrested for the actions of the provocateurs.

PEOPLE FALL into the trap of being provoked and thus continue the provoked actions. The chaos created makes it more challenging to find the root cause. The deeper issue and intention is to cause further mistrust and segregation.

NOTES ON UMBRELLA MAN

During the MPLS riots, an Umbrella Man video popped up on the internet the same day. The video showed a man in black riot gear carrying an umbrella on a clear day, intent on blocking the surrounding cameras from seeing his face. Some believed he was the one who threw the first brick. That video inspired this poem. (See the above note for similar commentary on this poem.)

NOTES ON MAY 3RD

I don't know how old this poem is or why it's titled May 3rd. I hope someday the date will unloose a deeper-connected memory for me. The image started when I was a kid with a particular old mirror in my bedroom. Maybe it was inspired by Alice in Wonderland, but I remember standing in front of this mirror and thinking that secrets could come through it- and they would be skeletons. The mirror sees everything.

THE POEM IS in this section because of the onomatopoeia within it. Lyrical and sound poems are often found in stories, movies, and poetry surrounding the macabre or comic books.

NOTES ON HALF THE MAN

Half the Man is my Biff Loman (*Death of a Salesman*, Arthur Miller) poem. I observed a gentleman traveling for work who stood in front of us at the car rental line.

I THOUGHT it odd that he came early on the weekend. I was young and hadn't traveled for work or conferences. I didn't know that this was common. My imagination took over and created the backstory about his life.

NOTES ON THE PROFESSOR

The professor is based on someone I've never met, but from what was described to me. He taught English at a community college, and he loved poetry. The poem is an homage to the theme of "a person reading poetry."

THE ESSENCE of *The Professor* is in the element of that which he loved most. So, even though this is about a specific person, it is an everyman professor who fully invests themself into the love of that which they teach.

NOTES ON WE ARE TIRED

What does weariness feel like? We all experience exhaustion, which at some point permeates every aspect of one's life. It can seem like there is no relief from it.

THE EVENTS that inspired *We Are Tired* happened during the Summer of 2020, but I have also felt it in times of grief and loneliness. Exhaustion like this is heavy. We can not add one more expectation or have one more thing for which we are responsible. We are sinking deep, our heads barely above water. In these moments, we need a hand to reach down and help us get out of it.

NOTES ON ARLINGTON

Walking at Arlington National Cemetery on Memorial Day 2008, I observed a bright Spring day full of singing birds. My Mother-in-law was fond of genealogy, which made her fascinated with cemeteries.

THAT DAY, there was a strange hush, except for the birds. It is odd to see such a restful place when so many died, knowing the harsh reality of war. The birds hopped from headstone to headstone, singing, almost as if declaring the deeds of the heroic dead.

LAMPLIGHTER

NOTES ON HEART TAX

Heart Tax is one of three Hindi-influenced poems (see below). Here's my shout-out to my Hindi teachers from Wattpad: @PretentiousWaffle and @Adairx. When you learn a language, you struggle with sound. This is why poetry is often difficult to translate into new languages, as sound often supports a poem's meaning.

I WANTED to use this poem to express one idea in two languages. This brief statement asks the reader: What is owed to the heart in love? What tax does your heart require?

NOTES ON A MOMENT IS CENTURIES

This is the second of three Hindi-influenced poems inspired by Bollywood long-burn romances. The first line is when the characters have all those unspoken feelings they refuse to share with the other. They are caught up by all their other responsibilities. In the end, they can not commit to loving each other. The pain becomes what they hold onto, reminding them that their love is real. It helps them get through the life they are living.

I UNDERSTAND that to any Hindi readers, it may not be a perfect representation of the language, but I hope you can forgive this student.

NOTES ON SUNSHINE AND MOON

Maybe love is like the moon and sun meeting. They cross between the setting and the rising of the day. It is a happy dance to travel hours until you meet again, and as they cross, there is a moment where they almost look like a heart. It is a brief meeting of a moment, but we travel the hours day after day, which accumulate into a life lived. It is a life well lived when spent in love.

PART THREE

ON WRITING

Writers write; it's what we do. I've observed my process, my thoughts, and what it looks like to create in this medium. I debated titling this part "A Writer's Lament," but alas, I did not.

In "Part Three: On Writing," you will read poems collected around the theme of a writer's internal struggle. Many poems in this part, or any other, could potentially fit another category. Still, I would like to think that each section says something together; each poem is part of a fuller conversation.

The craft of writing can be dangerous. Some say it's more dangerous than the sword. It is so dangerous that it carries the attribution of starting the French Revolution. It is a weighty gift, both dangerous as it is creative.

PAPAYA

Sometimes--
Writing is like fighting
with two fists against the air.

Sometimes--
like eating papaya,
pulpy, exotic,
frustrating, filling, and juicy.

Sometimes blank --
like now.

(February 27, 2003)

DILIGENCE

Diligence,
uncommon to me.

I sit
   as if forced to say
      something
         of importance
         of substance
         of worth.

Will I?
   look back,
      see something
         of inexperience
         of blindness
         of weakness

These abandoned words
   left to scream my name--

> they say,
> "You left us."
> "Here we sit
> because you forgot."

(April 14, 2000)

STORIES

Stories spill out of me--

"I know. I want to stab you."

Knife cuts deep.
Words drip into a bucket.

"But those are my own." I say.

I am ignored.
The bucket is full and carried away.

My hand holds my side.
My voice is gone when I cry out.

Infringement.

MEAL FOR BABY

I mash my words
   with melted butter.
I feed baby
   a forkful at a time.
I convince baby
   to swallow
  with bubbling
   airplane sounds,
a slight distraction
    to feed peas with
     that rolls about the tongue.
My thoughts I cut
    into bite size pieces.
Baby's full
    and doesn't like them,
    so, they end up on the floor.

LOVE

When in fact we love.
I see the many ways
that love breaks.
Love when splintered like wood,
leaves a weakened
structure behind.
We are a miracle.

WE DOUBT

Goodnight, victim of self-doubt.
Sleep buried deep under
armors of flesh.
Some time you can rise
when check meets
the middle ground.
We can deliberate then.

MOUTHPIECE

Beauty is a mouthpiece
manipulated,
a distorted view like
a kaleidoscope I arrange.

Truth is simmering
below the surface
and shimmering
above.

Turn up the heat
and let the kettle boil.
The china floral patterned
—cups are set.

Steep the tea for 5 minutes,
darling.
Too long and it becomes bitter.

LEVEZ-VOUS

Levez-vous mes amis.

Take up your pen.

It's time to shake

the world awake.

Shake the earth
with your words today.

INK

Ink on leaves
Summer hordes the green
speaking out

NOT GOODBYE

She led with a love
for words, and spent them
in vision, laying before friends
a feast.

A banquet of passion
she bequeathed.

Led not astray, but something
internal grew and built a nest
called home

where every care and corner
felt loved

until one day a new road
was paved further on.

The risk of a new road, an untraveled road
left so many questions to be answered.

S. A. MCNUTT

The thrill to seek (dare not retreat)
passions long dormant,
expressions still lingering
on a tree ripe with dripping fruit.
It is time to feast, friends
and revel in the time together.
Tomorrow brings light growing,
blossoming with promises new.

(May 25, 2020)

HAMMER AND NAIL

Hammer and nail together built the house.
The Northern woods supplied the lumber.
Young, strapping saplings lean in years—
Row by row leaning together joined board and
 beam.

Solid work of days withstands the treading of
 years,
of winds and rains yet to come.

And when every board leaned together,
and hammer left nail embedded,
when the work of each was done to completion,
 the door opened to take its first breath.

And when they crossed the threshold to call it
 home, it lived.

AUTHOR NOTES

PART THREE

NOTES ON PAPAYA

Inspired by Pablo Neruda's love poems, the poem *Papaya* drips and oozes words and meaning. The way Neruda used fruit in his poems, you could almost taste it.

THE OVERFLOWING FRUIT creates tension with the nothingness of the blank page. The writer often fights with stories not yet realized. They exist in the mind but are like punching air. You can't always get words on the page.

NOTES ON DILIGENCE

Do you have abandoned words, thoughts, or ideas that were never pursued to their fullness? I continue to drop off in the middle of writing something. It isn't easy to get back to the story, edit, or finish the story, poem, or book (like this one).

There are so many things that get in the way. I live this poem everyday.

I BELIEVE I am not alone in this frustration. I suspect that many artists and writers feel this way. The question is, should we embrace it? What would we finish if we embraced abandoning it? Maybe we would only finish our best work, the ones we emotionally connect to best. Perhaps I am just afraid of conclusions. I am comforted by the "never-ending story."

NOTES ON STORIES

For those who have experienced copyright infringement, this poem is for you. What would it look like for a thief to steal the author's work from body and soul? Stolen words are then taken out of context, misunderstood, and used for unintended purposes.

WHAT ABOUT WHEN artists are expected to give away their work for free? Or when the original artist isn't credited for their work because they aren't famous. They are ghostwriting under someone else's fame. No, instead, the great silencing of the writer begins, words dripping in a bucket. Soon, the writer is left without a voice.

NOTES ON MEAL FOR BABY

How can we make our work more palatable and more marketable? We try to make our work better suited for the world, to lull the world and make everything seem safe. Poetry can be joyous and lifting, but it can also be dangerous. The bravest poets in the world were sharpened swords unsheathed.

NOTES ON LOVE

Love is a brief reflection on its being a miracle. Love is a struggle but also a miracle. When you experience it and give in to it, you are experiencing the miracle for yourself.

NOTES ON WE DOUBT

Doubt is easy. I find it difficult to move past it and see the potential beyond. I recognize a need to deal with it, to prepare myself to wrestle with it and set it aside until I can face it. I never want to let it get in the way.

NOTES ON MOUTHPIECE

There is power in our words. This poem explores a similar theme to Emily Dickinson's poem about beauty and truth or her poem about truth being like slanted light. Images of beauty can be confused with truth. People will believe it because it's beautiful. The two ideas are close to each other, which is why marketers use beautiful people to sell products. You are inclined to trust them.

Our words and how we arrange them have power. Let truth come before beauty; it is already well adorned.

NOTES ON LEVEZ-VOUS

One of the brilliant things about Wattpad is the cross-cultural experience. There is great access to authors writing in other languages. This poem, among a few others, is a nod at my attempt to engage in different languages. The idea of *Levez-Vous* is to rise up. It is a call to use your words boldly and make them impactful.

NOTES ON INK

My little haiku, *Ink,* references a wonderful man who brought writing to his people. His name was Sequoyah. He created the Cherokee alphabet in written form in 1821. The story is that he watched soldiers reading sheets of paper (he compared them to leaves). He observed their reactions (laughing or crying) while reading the papers as if they were conversing. My poem hints at this connection in honor of Sequoyah, who had a love for communication between his people.

NOTES ON NOT GOODBYE

Sometimes, we are comfortable in our lives, not wanting anything to change, but often, when we explore the world of ideas, the life poetic, there is the risk that something deeper will start to itch within our souls. That itch can lead us to places we never imagined, new places to call home, more education, new hobbies, travel, and new careers. Sometimes, it leads to all those things.

NOTES ON HAMMER AND NAIL

Have you ever been in an empty house? When we purchased our home, it was empty the first time we visited it, and it felt cold. It was just walls and floors, doors and windows.

THE MOMENT we began to put furniture into it, it felt like it came alive. It is alive with us; every breath we take into it fills the house's lungs. It feels like home, something more alive because we live within it.

ACKNOWLEDGMENTS

To my parents, you gave me a childhood on a beautiful lake. You allowed me to be creative and never stifled the off-kilter way I saw the world. It is this that became the stuff of my poetry.

To Fatimah, Peter, and Cindy. After all these years, for all our conversations that helped grow my mind and thinking, for the years of meeting weekly, thank you for embracing my oddness.

To Yvonne, I am grateful to have your support as editor. Your thoughtful insight and encouragement kept the work moving forward. You are the real reason I got to this spot in the end. Your editorial sensitivity and challenges were all on point.

To our dog Pumpkin, thank you! Pumpkin, we miss you terribly. You always checked up on me when I was working. I miss that.

To my husband and best friend, Donnie, without whom I wouldn't be able to write at all. Your generosity of hard work and support has made this book possible. You are my favorite person. I love you!

And to God, my unending gratitude to you in all things. I would not be if You had not created me and formed me in my mother's womb or protected me from so many life dangers and snares.

Nothing is worthy and good if it isn't from you. You are first and foremost in all things. I offer out of myself, which begins and ends in you. Baruch ata Adonai!

ABOUT THE AUTHOR

S. A. McNutt is an emerging author. This is her first book of poetry cultivated over many years.

www.ingramcontent.com/pod-product-compliance
Lightning Source LLC
Chambersburg PA
CBHW070314010526
44107CB00004B/343